The
Original
Alice

Alice's Adventures under Ground

The Original Alice

FROM
MANUSCRIPT TO
WONDERLAND

Sally Brown

THE BRITISH LIBRARY

THE Reverend Charles Lutwidge Dodgson – later to be celebrated throughout the world as Lewis Carroll, author of *Alice's Adventures in Wonderland* – was a twenty-four year old mathematics lecturer at Christ Church, Oxford, when he first encountered Alice Liddell and her sisters, the small daughters of the new Dean of the cathedral college. [I] Dean Liddell, a former headmaster of Westminster School and chaplain to Prince Albert, was an eminent classical scholar, co-compiler of the monumental Greek-English Lexicon and, in his friend John Ruskin's words, `one of the rarest types of nobly presenced Englishmen'. When he and his wife, Lorina, arrived at the Deanery in 1855 they brought with them their four children, Harry, Lorina, Alice and Edith; four more – two girls and two boys – were to be born in Oxford.

Dodgson himself was the third child and eldest son in a family of seven girls and four boys, and had always taken pleasure in children's company. Brought up with his lively, affectionate brothers and sisters in a Yorkshire rectory, he revealed at an early age the talent for story-telling, jokes, riddles, elaborate games and entertainments which was to enthrall his `child-friends', as he called them, throughout his life. In 1853, two years after his arrival in Oxford as an undergraduate, he began to keep a diary, a habit which continued until his death forty-five years later. Four volumes of his diaries are lost, but

1 Photograph of Dodgson by Reginald Southey, *c.*1856

the nine which have survived are now in the British Library; it is through them that we are able to chart the course of the most important of these friendships, which eventually led to the writing of the 'fairy tale' that was to become *Alice's Adventures in Wonderland*.

In Dodgson's diary entry for 6 March 1856 we find the first mention of his having made the acquaintance of 'little Harry Liddell ... certainly the handsomest boy I ever saw'; two days later he relates that, at a musical party in the Deanery, he 'took the opportunity of making friends with Lorina ... the second of the family.' It was not until the following term, however, that he met Alice, who was then just under four years old, and the smallest sister, Edith. On 25 April 1856 he went with his friend Reginald Southey to the Deanery, to try – with a borrowed camera – to take a photograph of the Cathedral. Two attempts to do so were unsuccessful, but his diary continues: 'The three little girls were in the garden most of the time, and we became excellent friends: we tried to group them in the foreground of the picture, but they were not patient sitters.' The entry concludes with the significant pronouncement, 'I mark this day with a white stone'; this, the Roman poet Catullus's symbol for a day of good fortune, was reserved by Dodgson for particularly memorable occasions.

Dodgson and Southey returned to the Deanery on three successive days during the following week, and succeeded in

2 Dodgson's nine surviving diaries

taking more photographs of the Liddell children. A small room next to the Library at Christ Church, which Dodgson occupied as sub-librarian, looks out over the lawn and flower beds of the garden where Harry and his sisters were often to be seen playing. On 10 May, Dodgson writes: 'I went over to the Library, and called to Harry Liddell from the window, and got him to come over to Southey's room. We had great difficulty in getting him to sit still long enough ... Southey succeeded at last, by placing him in a bright light, in getting a fair profile.' A few days later, he proudly took Harry's photograph over to the Deanery and was invited to stay to lunch. The Dean, himself a photography enthusiast, was impressed with Dodgson's work and this occasion marked the beginning of a period of frequent comings and goings between the shy, stuttering don and the lively, intelligent young Liddells. As the friendship grew, photography sessions were interspersed with croquet, puppet shows and plays, conjuring performances, long walks and river picnics.

When collodion wet-plate photography became available to the public in 1855, Dodgson, who had been interested in drawing and painting from his youth, was immediately attracted to this new art form. It was an extremely complicated and exacting business: cameras were large and clumsy, pictures had to be taken in bright daylight and sitters were compelled to hold a pose for a long time. As Dodgson himself declared in his poem 'Hiawatha's Photographing', 'Mystic, awful was the process.' When he first started experimenting with photography he took pictures of family, friends and colleagues, and he tried some architectural and landscape subjects. His most successful photographs, however, were of children – especially little girls, in whose company his habitual stammer would 'softly and suddenly vanish away', like the subject of his famous poem 'The Hunting of the Snark'. Thoroughly methodical by nature, he kept a register of the names and ages of all the children he photographed, with the date and number of the negative. The fact that he is now acclaimed as one of the most successful and imaginative Victorian photographers is due not merely to his technical skills but his natural ability to charm and entertain his sitters.

Dodgson first photographed the Liddell children with his own camera on 3 June 1856. Many years later, in 1932, Alice recalled that she and her sisters never resented having to sit still for a long time as he took their photograph, because of the wonderful stories he would tell them as he did so, 'illustrating them by pencil and ink drawings as he went along'. 'When we were thoroughly happy and amused at his stories,' she wrote, 'he used to pose us, and expose the plates, before the right mood had passed. He seemed to have an endless fund of fantastical stories, which he made up as he told them ...'. [3] In some of the most beguiling of Dodgson's photographs of the three girls together, they are dressed up in costume. He loved theatricals of all kinds; a cupboard in his college rooms was full of dressing-up clothes, some bought from pantomime sales, including a Turkish outfit, a Greek dress and a suit of mail. Occasionally he would send his 'scout' (as college servants are called in Oxford) over to the Ashmolean Museum for some more exotic or unusual item of clothing. A native cloak and anklet were procured in this way for the small daughter of the Professor of Sanskrit, who was to be portrayed as a sleeping savage.

Dodgson's photographic skills soon began to attract admirers in Oxford and further afield. Queen Victoria's son, the Prince of Wales, who was an undergraduate at Christ Church during this period, singled out his portrayal of Lorina and Alice dressed as Chinamen for particular praise; [4] the Poet Laureate, Alfred Tennyson, was so entranced by a photograph of Alice posing as a ragged beggar girl that he declared it the most beautiful portrait of a child he had ever seen. [5] From the first, Alice was Dodgson's favourite, and his photographs of her possess a special, almost haunting quality. She was a charming and very pretty child with short, straight dark hair cut in a fringe, large blue eyes and a strikingly gentle and innocent face; in later years Dodgson always preferred to remember her as 'an entirely fascinating seven-year-old maiden'. Like the heroine of her 'adventures', she was

3 Photograph by Dodgson
of Alice, Lorina and Edith Liddell, 1859

full of intelligent curiosity, and loved reading. Of the many photographs of her on her own, one of the most simple and successful shows her in pensive profile, sitting on a high-backed wooden chair. [6] Dodgson was constantly thinking of new ideas to please her, summoning up his best stories, puzzles and jokes, and was desolate on the rare occasions when she did not respond with her usual cheerfulness and enthusiasm. In a letter of February 1861 to his sister Mary, he reports: 'My small friends the Liddells are all in the measles just now. I met them yesterday. Alice ... looked awfully melancholy – it was almost impossible to make her smile ...'.

Alice herself recalled in old age the happy days she and her sisters spent in Dodgson's company: 'He used sometimes to come to the Deanery on the afternoons when we had a half holiday ... On the other hand, when we went on the river for the afternoon with Mr Dodgson ... he always brought with him a large basket full of cakes, and a kettle, which we used to boil under a haycock, if we could find one. On rarer occasions we went out for the whole day with him, and then we took a larger basket with luncheon ... One of our favourite whole-day excursions was to row down to Nuneham and picnic in the woods there ... Sometimes we were told stories after luncheon that transported us into Fairyland ... On these occasions we did not get home until seven o'clock.'

Nuneham, with its landscaped park and deep, mysterious

4 Photograph by Dodgson
of Alice and Lorina in Chinese costume

5 Photograph by Dodgson
of Alice dressed as a beggar girl, 1858 (hand-coloured)

woods, provided the ideal destination for a day's outing. Five miles downstream from Oxford, it was just the right distance away and in the easiest direction for the children to row. In her reminiscences, Alice described their rowing lessons in some detail: 'After we had chosen our boat with great care, we three children were stowed away in the stern, and Mr Dodgson took the stroke oar ... He succeeded in teaching us in the course of these excursions, and it proved an unending joy ... When we had learned enough to manage the oars, we were allowed to take our turn at them ... I can remember what hard work it was rowing upstream from Nuneham, but this was nothing if we thought we were learning and getting on. It was a proud day when we could "feather our oars" properly.' Dodgson himself captures his delight in these river trips, and the children's eager attempts at rowing, in the first stanza of the prefatory poem to *Alice's Adventures in Wonderland*:

All in the golden afternoon
Full leisurely we glide;
For both our oars, with little skill,
By little arms are plied,
While little hands make vain pretence
Our wanderings to guide

On 17 June 1862, Dodgson's diary records a river expe-

6 Photograph by Dodgson of Alice in profile, 1859

dition which included his sisters Fanny and Elizabeth and his aunt Lucy, who were visiting him at the time, and his friend Robinson Duckworth, a Fellow of Trinity College who later went on to become Chaplain to the Queen and Canon of Westminster. It turned into an unexpected adventure:

'Expedition to Nuneham. Duckworth ... and Ina, Alice and Edith came with us. We ... got to Nuneham about 2: dined there, walked in the park, and set off for home about 4½. About a mile above Nuneham heavy rain came on, and after bearing it a short time I settled that we had better leave the boat and walk: 3 miles of this drenched us all pretty well. I went on first with the children, as they could walk much faster than Elizabeth, and took them to the only house I knew in Sandford ... I left them ... to get their clothes dried, and went off to find a vehicle, but none was to be had there ... Duckworth and I walked on to Iffley, whence we sent them a fly. We all had tea in my rooms, about 8½, after which I took the children home ...'

The unexpected drenching that day later inspired the extraordinary 'pool of tears' episode in the *Alice* story, where the party is recast as a congregation of birds: Lorina becomes the Lory, Edith the Eaglet, Duckworth the Duck, and – in a wry reference to his stammer – Dodgson himself is portrayed as the solemn and portentous Dodo. [7]

Another trip to Nuneham was planned on 3 July, but rain prevented it. The next day was fine, however, and the three

7 Dodgson's illustration of Alice with a crowd of creatures
in the 'pool of tears'

girls – then thirteen, ten and eight years old – set out with
Dodgson on an expedition which was destined to make literary history. They left the Deanery after lunch, dressed as
usual in white cotton dresses, wide-brimmed hats, white socks
and black buttoned shoes. Their governess, the formidably-
named Miss Prickett, walked with them as far as Dodgson's
rooms in the Old Library, and left them there in the care of
Dodgson and Duckworth, who was to accompany them once
again; the children were greatly taken with his charm, sense
of humour and fine singing voice. With the men carrying the
picnic-baskets, the party made its way through Christ Church

Meadow to Folly Bridge, where they chose their boat and set off upstream for a change. Dodgson's diary entry records: 'Duckworth and I made an expedition *up* the river to Godstow with the 3 Liddells: we had tea on the bank there, and did not reach Christ Church again until ½ past 8, when we took them on to my rooms to see my collection of microphotographs, and restored them to the Deanery just before 9.' On the opposite page is a note dated 10 February 1863: 'On which occasion I told them the fairy-tale of "Alice's Adventures Under Ground", which I undertook to write out for Alice, and which is now finished ... .' [8]

Duckworth later recalled this momentous day: 'I rowed *stroke* and he rowed *bow* in the famous Long Vacation voyage to Godstow, when the three Miss Liddells were our passengers, and the story was actually composed and spoken *over my shoulder* for the benefit of Alice Liddell, who was acting as "cox" of our gig. I remember turning round and saying, "Dodgson, is this an extempore romance of yours?" And he replied, "Yes, I'm inventing as we go along."' Duckworth also remembered Alice begging his friend, on the children's return to the Deanery, to write out this particularly enthralling story for her, and Dodgson's claim that he had then stayed up nearly all night, 'committing to a MS book his recollections of the drolleries with which he had enlivened the afternoon'.

Whether or not Dodgson actually worked for most of that

night, as Duckworth declared, his diary for the next day records that on the train up to London, where he was going to see the 1862 Exhibition, he wrote out the 'headings' of 'Alice's Adventures Under Ground'. Twenty-five years later, in an article for *The Theatre*, he described the 'golden afternoon' that inspired the famous tale: '... the cloudless blue above, the watery mirror below, the boat drifting idly on its way, the tinkle of the drops that fell from the oars, as they waved so sleepily to and fro, and ... the three eager faces ... from whose lips "Tell us a story, please" had all the stern immutability of Fate!' He also recalled that, 'in a desperate attempt to strike out some new line of fairy-lore', he had sent Alice 'straight down a rabbit-hole, to begin with, without the least idea what was to happen afterwards'. Many of the subsequent happenings were, in fact, inspired by particular Oxford events, characters and situations which, though strongly tinged with fantasy, would have been instantly recognisable to the children. Alice later recalled that her 'frequent interruptions' would open up 'fresh and undreamed of possibilities' as the story progressed.

On I August 1862, Dodgson heard the three Liddells sing 'Beautiful Star', a popular song by J.M. Sayles. This is parodied in the 'Turtle Soup' song of the *Alice* story; its plaintive refrain, 'Soup of the evening, beautiful soup!', is sung by the Mock Turtle with an amusingly exaggerated air of

8 Dodgson's diary entry for 4 July 1862

July 4 (F) Atkinson brought over to
my rooms some friends of his, a Mrs
& Miss Peters, of whom I took photographs,
& who afterwards looked over my albums
& staid to lunch. They then went off
to the Museum, & Duckworth & I
made an expedition up the river to
Godstow with the 3 Liddells : we
had tea on the bank there, & did
not reach Ch. Ch. again till ¼
past 8, when we took them on to
my rooms to see my collection of
micro-photographs, & restored them to
the Deanery, just before 9

July 5 (Sat.) Left, with Atkinson,
for London at 9·2, meeting at the
station the Liddells, who went by the
same train. We reached 4. Alfred
Place about 11, & found Aunt L. P. J.,
& E. L. there, & took the 2 last to see
Marochetti's studio. After luncheon
Atkinson left, & we visited the Inter-
national Bazaar.

melancholy. [9] A few days later he took the children on another trip to Godstow, during which, he wrote in his diary, 'I had to go on with my interminable fairy-tale of *Alice's Adventures*'. On the Liddell family's return from their annual seaside holiday, however, Dodgson's meetings with the three sisters became less frequent. Mrs Liddell may have felt that his friendship with her daughters was becoming too close; when he came across Lorina, Alice and Edith in the college quadrangle on 13 November, he commented in his diary that this was 'a rare event of late'. Perhaps Alice reminded him of his promise to write down her 'adventures' on this occasion, for the entry continues: 'Began writing the fairy-tale for Alice, which I told them July 4th, going to Godstow – I hope to finish it by Christmas.' By this he presumably means the formal manuscript he was preparing, since the 'headings' and rough notes were already in existence. He had finished writing this out in his neat 'manuscript print' hand, using sepia-coloured ink, by February 1863, but it took him much longer to finish the 'pen and ink pictures ... of my own devising' with which he had decided to embellish it.

1863 was, in fact, to be the last year in which Dodgson continued to see Alice with any regularity. In March he received a letter from her in French, asking him to accompany her to the grand and elaborate 'illuminations' held in Oxford to celebrate the marriage of the Prince of Wales and

9 The 'Beautiful Soup' page
from 'Alice's Adventures Under Ground'

"Thank you," said Alice, feeling very glad that the figure was over.

"Shall we try the second figure?" said the Gryphon, "or would you prefer a song?"

"Oh, a song, please!" Alice replied, so eagerly, that the Gryphon said, in a rather offended tone, "hm! no accounting for tastes! Sing her 'Mock Turtle Soup', will you, old fellow!"

The Mock Turtle sighed deeply, and began, in a voice sometimes choked with sobs, to sing this:

"Beautiful Soup, so rich and green,
Waiting in a hot tureen!
Who for such dainties would not stoop?
Soup of the evening, beautiful Soup!
Soup of the evening, beautiful Soup!
      Beau — ootiful Soo — oop!
      Beau — ootiful Soo — oop!
Soo — oop of the e — e — evening,
      Beautiful beautiful Soup!

"Chorus again!" cried the Gryphon, and

2

Chapter 1.

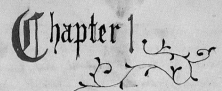

Alice was beginning to get very tired of sitting by her sister on the bank, and of having nothing to do: once or twice she had peeped into the book her sister was reading, but it had no pictures or conversations in it, and where is the use of a book, thought Alice, without pictures or conversations? So she was considering in her own mind, (as well as she could, for the hot day made her feel very sleepy and stupid,) whether the pleasure of making a daisy-chain was worth the trouble of getting up and picking the daisies, when a white rabbit with pink eyes ran close by her.

There was nothing very remarkable in that, nor did Alice think it so very much out of the way to hear the rabbit say to itself "dear, dear! I shall be too late!" (when she thought it over afterwards, it occurred to her that she ought to have wondered at this, but at the time it all seemed quite natural); but when the rabbit actually took a watch out of its waistcoat-pocket, looked at it, and then hurried on, Alice started to her feet, for

Princess Alexandra (a 'white stone' day); in April he joined the Liddell children on a visit to their grandmother, who lived near Cheltenham; in May he presented Alice with a book as an eleventh birthday present; in June there were more river picnics (now, however, with Miss Prickett in attendance), the exciting preparations for the visit to Christ Church of the newlywed Prince and Princess, a bazaar, and a trip to the circus. On 25 June Dodgson joined a large Liddell family river outing to Nuneham which ended in his taking Alice and her sisters back to Oxford by train: 'a pleasant expedition,' he wrote in his diary, 'with a very pleasant conclusion'.

Immediately after this episode, a crisis occurred in Dodgson's relations with the family, causing a break with the Dean and Mrs Liddell and cutting him off from the children for some months. We do not know the precise nature of this crisis because, many years later, Dodgson's niece, Menella, cut out the page of his diary containing entries for 27, 28 and 29 June. Some surviving notes made by her suggest that it might have arisen from Oxford gossip about Dodgson's paying too much attention to Lorina, now rapidly developing into a beautiful young woman. Clearly, he was deeply upset and offended by whatever had occurred between him and the Liddells, for on 2 December he wrote in his diary that he had seen the children with their mother, 'but I held aloof from them, as I have done all this term'. Even before this rift arose,

10 The opening page of 'Alice's Adventures Under Ground'

A Christmas Gift
to
a Dear Child
in Memory
of
a Summer Day.

however, it was plain that Mrs Liddell, who had high social ambitions for her daughters, did not always welcome Dodgson's friendship with them. Although the atmosphere gradually thawed, his relationship with Alice and her sisters never returned to its former ease and closeness; by May 1865, he was sufficiently estranged from Alice to comment after a chance meeting that she had 'changed a good deal, and hardly for the better ...'.

The manuscript of 'Alice's Adventures Under Ground' was finally dispatched to Alice, as an early Christmas present, on 26 November 1864. It was bound as a little book of ninety pages, in dark green morocco leather, with a beautifully designed and coloured title page and the slightly wistful dedication, 'To a dear child, in memory of a summer day' [11]. The thirty-seven illustrations – fourteen of them full-page – had taken a long time to complete, and caused Dodgson, who was completely untrained as an artist, a certain amount of anguish. He borrowed a natural history book from the Deanery to help with the animal subjects; the infinite trouble he took over the task can be seen in the pages of trial sketches preserved in the library at Christ Church. Some of the comic drawings in the manuscript (for instance, those illustrating 'You are old, Father William', a parody of a poem by Robert Southey) are reminiscent of Edward Lear, whose *Book of Nonsense* was published in 1846; they also recall

11 Dedication page from 'Alice's Adventures Under Ground'

Dodgson's lively childhood sketches for the family magazines, with such titles as *The Rectory Umbrella* and *Mischmasch*, which he wrote for the amusement of his siblings. [12] Several of his illustrations of the long-haired Alice (he had decided that the story's heroine should not physically resemble his 'ideal child-friend') possess a distinctly Pre-Raphaelite quality: the full-page illustration of a magically expanded Alice trapped in the White Rabbit's house, for instance, was inspired by a Dante Gabriel Rossetti print, and her pose, with head inclined, holding the 'little magic bottle' (the contents of which had caused her to grow suddenly taller) was taken from Arthur Hughes's painting *The Lady with the Lilacs*, which Dodgson owned. [14, 15] He was a great admirer of this group of artists, and had photographed several of them.

At the very end of his little book, Dodgson made a small head and shoulders drawing of the 'real' Alice at the age of seven, carefully copied from a photograph. This charming image is, in fact, his only surviving drawing of her, but he must have been dissatisfied with it because he then pasted the oval photograph on top. The original sketch was not discovered until 1977, when the Canadian scholar (and now Dodgson's biographer) Morton Cohen closely examined the manuscript on a visit to the British Library. Convinced that something lay beneath the photograph, he persuaded the conservation staff to lift it. An ingenious paper hinge now allows the two

12 Dodgson's illustration
and two verses from the 'Father William' poem

3.

"You are old," said the youth, "as I mentioned before,
  "And have grown most uncommonly fat:
Yet you turned a back-somersault in at the door—
  Pray what is the reason of that?"

4.

"In my youth," said the sage, as he shook his gray locks,
  "I kept all my limbs very supple.
By the use of this ointment, five shillings the box—
  Allow me to sell you a couple."

how she was ever to get out again: suddenly
she came upon a little three-legged table,
all made of solid glass; there was nothing
lying upon it, but a tiny golden key, and
Alice's first idea was that it might belong
to one of the doors of the hall, but alas! either
the locks were too large,
or the key too small, but
at any rate it would open
none of them. However, on
the second time round, she
came to a low curtain,
behind which was a door
about eighteen inches high:
she tried the little key in
the keyhole, and it fitted! Alice opened the door,
and looked down a small passage, not larger
than a rat-hole, into the loveliest garden you
ever saw. How she longed to get out of that
dark hall, and wander about among those beds
of bright flowers and those cool fountains, but
she could not even get her head through the
doorway, "and even if my head would go through,"
thought poor Alice, "it would be very little use
without my shoulders. Oh, how I wish I could shut

images to be seen one on top of the other. [16, 17]

When Dodgson had finished writing out the text of 'Alice's Adventures Under Ground', he lent it to a friend, the children's novelist George MacDonald, whose opinion he trusted, and whose 1858 fairy tale, *Phantastes*, he particularly admired. Mrs MacDonald read it aloud to her children, to their great delight. Years later, her son Greville wrote: 'I remember that first reading well, and also my braggart avowal that I wished there were sixty thousand volumes of it!' Dodgson's diary entry for 9 May 1863 includes the announcement that 'They wish me to publish.' Once the finished manuscript was installed at the Deanery, where visitors were invited to admire it, Henry Kingsley, novelist brother of the author of *The Water Babies*, was so taken with the story that he insisted that Mrs Liddell urge Dodgson to consider its publication. By this time, however, the process was already underway. Dodgson later wrote that 'there was no idea of publication in my mind when I wrote this little book; *that* was wholly an afterthought, pressed on me by the "perhaps too partial friends" who always have to bear the blame when an author rushes into print.'

As soon as he began to contemplate publication, Dodgson realised that the original story would have to be fleshed out with more incidents and characters. Some of the private Liddell family jokes and references were removed, as was the

13 Dodgson's illustration of Alice with the 'tiny golden key'

than she expected: before she had drunk
half the bottle, she found her head pressing
against the ceiling, and she stooped to save
her neck from being broken, and hastily
put down the bottle, saying to herself "that's
quite enough—
I hope I sha'n't
grow any more—
I wish I hadn't
drunk so much!"

Alas! it
was too late:
she went on
growing and
growing, and very
soon had to
kneel down: in
another minute there was not room even for
this, and she tried the effect of lying
down, with one elbow against the door,
and the other arm curled round her
head. Still she went on growing, and as
a last resource she put one arm out of
the window, and one foot up the chimney,
and said to herself "now I can do no
more — what will become of me?"

14 and 15
Alice with the
'little magic
bottle' and in
the White
Rabbit's
house

of her own little sister. So the boat wound slowly along, beneath the bright summer-day, with its merry crew and its music of voices and laughter, till it passed round one of the many turnings of the stream, and she saw it no more.

Then she thought, (in a dream within the dream, as it were,) how this same little Alice would, in the after-time, be herself a grown woman: and how she would keep, through her riper years, the simple and loving heart of her childhood: and how she would gather around her other little children, and make their eyes bright and eager with many a wonderful tale, perhaps even with these very adventures of the little Alice of long-ago: and how she would feel with all their simple sorrows, and find a pleasure in all their simple joys, remembering her own child-life, and the happy summer-days. days.

16
The final page of the manuscript, showing Dodgson's drawing of Alice

of her own little sister. So the boat wound slowly along, beneath the bright summer-day, with its merry crew and its music of voices and laughter, till it passed round one of the many turnings of the stream, and she saw it no more.

Then she thought, (in a dream within the dream, as it were,) how this same little Alice would, in the after-time, be herself a grown woman: and how she would keep, through her riper years, the simple and loving heart of her childhood; and how she would gather around her other little children, and make *their* eyes bright and eager with many a wonderful tale, perhaps even with these very adventures of the little Alice of long-ago: and how she would feel with all their simple sorrows, and find a pleasure in all their simple joys, remembering her own child-life, and the happy summer

47

17
The final page
of the
manuscript,
showing the
photograph of
Alice

lyrical passage at the very end of the story which describes 'an ancient city, and a quiet river winding near it along the plain'. As he later explained, the first, more private version of Alice's adventures was 're-written, and enlarged', eventually growing from 18,000 to 35,000 words; two completely new chapters, 'Pig and Pepper' and 'A Mad Tea-Party', were added, and the final trial scene was greatly expanded to incorporate some of the new characters, including the Hatter, with his companions the March Hare and the Dormouse, and the Duchess's fierce, pepper-dispensing cook.

Despite these changes and additions, however, many allusions to people and places that were familiar to Alice and her sisters remain embedded in the published story. The three little girls in the Dormouse's rambling account of the 'treacle well', Elsie, Lacie and Tillie, are the three Liddells in disguise: Elsie stands for L. C., the initials of Lorina Charlotte; Lacie is an anagram of Alice; and Matilda ('Tillie') was a family nickname for Edith. The lessons described by the Mock Turtle and Gryphon are a joking allusion to the children's experiences at the hands of Miss Prickett and several other masters and mistresses who tried to teach them 'extras', including the Quadrille, transformed in Dodgson's version into a solemn dance of sea creatures. The poem 'Twinkle twinkle little bat' is thought to refer to Professor Bartholomew Price, whom the children nicknamed 'Bat', and

18 Dodgson's illustration
of Alice standing before a door in a tree

the inspiration for the Hatter is alleged to have been Theophilus Carter, an eccentric Oxford furniture dealer.

Although he had used local presses for printing small pamphlets, Dodgson now needed a proper London publisher, and found one in Alexander Macmillan, introduced to him by an Oxford friend in October 1863. Macmillan was delighted by the story, and the two men entered into a commission agreement: Dodgson would bear the expenses of publishing his book and Macmillan would receive a percentage of the gross profits for producing and distributing it. During the course of its production they established a close working relationship. Dodgson bombarded Macmillan with letters about every aspect of the book's content and appearance; on 11 November 1864, for instance, he declared: 'I have been considering the question of the *colour* of *Alice's Adventures* and have come to the conclusion that *bright red* will be the best – not the best, perhaps, artistically, but the most attractive to childish eyes ...'.

Once he had settled on a publisher, Dodgson's next step – having decided, rather reluctantly, that his own drawings were not professional enough – was to find an illustrator for his story. Duckworth suggested John Tenniel, an acclaimed artist with a talent for drawing animals, whose work appeared regularly in the comic magazine *Punch*, which Dodgson enjoyed reading. On 20 December 1863, two months after his first meeting with Macmillan, he wrote to his friend Tom Taylor, a dramatist and critic (and later editor of *Punch*), asking him if he knew Tenniel well enough 'to say whether he could undertake such a thing as drawing a dozen wood-cuts to illustrate a child's book'. 'The reasons for which I ask,' Dodgson continued, ' ... are that I have written such a tale for a young friend, and illustrated it in pen and ink. It has been read and liked by so many children, and I have been so often asked to publish it, that I have decided on so doing ...'.

A month later, Dodgson called on Tenniel in London, armed with Taylor's letter of introduction. He found the artist 'receptive' to the idea of 'undertaking the pictures', though he delayed his final decision until he had seen the manuscript. Tenniel was invited to Oxford to explore the background to the story, the familiar scenes and objects which Dodgson had, consciously or unconsciously, woven into his fantastic tale of Alice's encounters with a variety of strange creatures and situations 'under ground'. Dodgson's diary entry for 12 October 1864 describes the early stages of their relationship, which was dogged by delays on Tenniel's part, often caused by the ceaseless weekly demands of *Punch*: 'Called on Macmillan and had some talk about the book ... Thence I went to Tenniel's, who showed me one drawing on wood ... of Alice sitting by the pool of tears, and the rabbit hurrying away – We discussed the book, and agreed on about 34

19 Tenniel's illustration of Alice in the 'pool of tears'

pictures ...'. Tenniel eventually produced seven more than this projected figure.

Some of the illustrations in *Alice's Adventures in Wonderland* are clearly based on Dodgson's original drawings (Alice swimming in the pool of tears, for instance), [19,20] but when he came to the new characters and episodes which appeared in the expanded story Tenniel had more of a free hand. His drawings of the Hatter, March Hare and Dormouse, and of the Duchess with her cook and baby, are brilliantly witty and accomplished. [21] The grinning Cheshire Cat, another com-

20 Dodgson's illustration of
Alice swimming in the 'pool of tears'

as she hurried back to the little door, but the little door was locked again, and the little gold key was lying on the glass table as before, and "things are worse than ever!" thought the poor little girl, "for I never was as small as this before, never! And I declare it's too bad, it is!"

At this moment her foot slipped, and splash! she was up to her chin in salt water. Her first idea was that she had fallen into the sea: then she remembered that she was under ground, and she soon made out that it was the pool of tears she had wept when she was nine feet high. "I wish I hadn't cried so much!" said Alice, as she swam about, trying to find her way out, "I shall be punished for it now, I suppose, by being drowned in my own tears! Well! that'll

21 Tenniel's illustration of the Hatter's tea-party

pletely new character, is shown in one of his drawings sitting on the branch of a tree very like the large chestnut tree in the Deanery garden, where Alice's own tabby cat, Dinah, was often to be found. [22] Alice herself, with her perfectly composed china doll features, has a far more grown-up air in Tenniel's illustrations than in Dodgson's occasionally awkward drawings of his seven-year-old heroine.

Dodgson's extreme perfectionism could make working with him at times a distinctly wearying experience. Christ Church Library still possesses his elaborate plan of the illustrations for the published book, showing exactly what size they should be and how they should be set into the text; several of his own designs for the title page and the opening of chapter one; carefully corrected proof pages; and his own pasted mock-up of the entirely new 'Mouse's Tail' poem (more overtly threatening in tone than the simple rhyme of the first version), which Macmillan's had originally set in a stiff, straight line instead of the required undulating curves. [23, 24] The exchanges between author and illustrator are not well documented: Tenniel probably destroyed Dodgson's letters and only a few brief notes from artist to author have survived. In the end, it was a mutual obsession with detail which helped to calm the occasional outbursts of anger and pique which arose throughout their collaboration. There can be no doubt, however, about the success of Tenniel's contribution to the published book; the peculiar charm of the story and its vivid, entrancing images is for most readers inseparable from his illustrations, which were expertly carved into woodblocks (now on permanent loan to the British Library) by the famous Dalziel brothers.

The British Library possesses a letter from Dodgson to Tom Taylor, dated 10 June 1864, in which he asks for help in 'fixing on a name for my fairy-tale'. He had decided that the original title was not sufficiently mysterious, enticing or magical. Several possibilities are listed: 'Alice among the

"But I don't want to go among mad people," Alice remarked.

"Oh, you ca'n't help that," said the Cat: "we're all mad here. I'm mad. You're mad."

"How do you know I'm mad?" said Alice.

"You must be," said the Cat, "or you wouldn't have come here."

Alice didn't think that proved it at all: how-

Elves/Goblins', 'Alice's Hour in Elfland' and 'Alice's Hour/Adventures in Wonderland', which Taylor liked best. The mention of goblins appears strange, since they do not feature in the published story, but grinning goblin faces are to be found in Dodgson's early sketches for the original version (for which no draft has survived), preserved at Christ Church. Also in the British Library is one of the very few surviving copies of the first edition of *Alice's Adventures in Wonderland*. [26] This appeared at long last at the end of June 1865, under the pseudonym 'Lewis Carroll' (an adaptation of his first two names), which Dodgson had used before in sending contributions to comic magazines. Two thousand copies were printed by the Clarendon Press; Dodgson inscribed 'twenty or more' as 'presents to various friends' and sent a special copy bound in white vellum to Alice at the Deanery, to mark the third anniversary of their famous river journey.

The first printing of the book is now known as the 'suppressed' edition. On 19 July Dodgson received a letter from Tenniel stating that he was 'entirely dissatisfied with the printing of the pictures' and so decided, with some anguish, that all existing copies should be withdrawn. Tenniel's complaint arose from the fact that nine of his illustrations appeared to be printed a little lighter, and another nine a little heavier, than he thought desirable. In cancelling the edition, Dodgson stood to lose a substantial amount of his own money; altogether, he had spent a

22 Tenniel's illustration of Alice with the Cheshire Cat

We lived beneath the mat
  Warm and snug and fat
    But one woe, & that
        Was the cat!
            To our joys
            a clog, In
            our eyes a
            fog, On our
          hearts a log
        Was the dog!
      When the
    cat's away,
  Then
  the mice
  will
  play,
    But, alas!
      one day, (So they say)
        Came the dog and
              cat, Hunting
                  for a
                  rat,
                Crushed
              the mice
            all flat,
          Each
          one
          as
          he
          sat
          Underneath the mat,
                      Warm & snug & fat — Think of that!

23
Dodgson's
illustration of
the original
'Mouse's Tail'
poem

24
(opposite)
The new
'Mouse's Tail'
poem

so that her idea of the tale was something like
this :—" Fury said to a

           mouse, That
            he met in the
              house, 'Let
                us both go
                  to law: *I*
                  will prose-
                  cute *you.*—
                Come, I 'll
              take no de-
            nial: We
          must have
        the trial;
     For really
    this morn-
   ing I've
  nothing
  to do.'
  Said the
   mouse to
    the cur,
     ' Such a
       trial, dear
         sir, With
           no jury
            or judge,
             would
             be wast-
            ing our
           breath.'
       'I 'll be
      judge,
    I'll be
   jury,'
  said
  cun-
  ning
  old
  Fury;
   'I 'll
    t r y
     the
      whole
      cause,
      and
     con-
     demn
    you to
death '."

25 Tenniel's illustration of Alice with the Dodo

26 The British Library's copy of the first edition of
Alice's Adventures in Wonderland

ALICE'S ADVENTURES

IN WONDERLAND.

BY

LEWIS CARROLL.

WITH FORTY-TWO ILLUSTRATIONS
BY JOHN TENNIEL.

London:
MACMILLAN AND CO.
1866.

total of £497 on the book (almost Tenniel's annual *Punch* salary), of which the artist received £138, the Dalziels £142 for their engravings, the printers £137 and the binders and advertisers £80. Nevertheless, he refused to compromise on its artistic quality, and respected Tenniel's objections.

Dodgson felt compelled to write to those friends who had already received copies to ask for their return, 'as the pictures are so badly done'. He engaged a new printer, Richard Clay of London, and the first copy of the new impression, although dated 1866, arrived at Christ Church on 9 November 1865. Tenniel kept him waiting almost a month before expressing his approval, at which point Dodgson felt free at last to praise the book; he declared in his diary that it was 'very *far* superior to the old, and in fact a perfect piece of artistic printing'. The question of disposing of the imperfect first edition – which he had initially thought of selling as waste paper in an attempt to recoup some of his losses – was resolved by selling the copies, at Tenniel's suggestion, to America, where they appeared that autumn, issued by Appleton of New York. Dodgson was further delighted by his original printer's magnanimous gesture in writing off the cost of the inferior printing. Little did he or Tenniel imagine that the few surviving English copies of the 'suppressed' edition would one day command huge sums of money and be fought over by book collectors.

Alice's Adventures in Wonderland was widely reviewed and received almost unconditional praise. Dodgson kept a careful record in his diary of the early notices. *The Reader* described it as 'a glorious artistic treasure', while the *Press* admired its 'simple and attractive style', judged it 'amusingly written' and declared that 'a child, when once the tale has commenced, will long to hear the whole of this wondrous narrative'. The *Publisher's Circular* selected it as 'the most original and the most charming' of the children's books sent to them that year, the *Bookseller* announced that 'a more original fairy tale ... it has not lately been our good fortune to read', and the *Guardian* thought it 'graceful' and 'full of humour'. Only the *Athenaeum* struck a different note: 'We fear that any child might be more puzzled than enchanted by this stiff, overwrought story.'

Sales of the book began steadily, and then rapidly increased. New editions appeared annually from 1866-68, Dodgson receiving a handsome profit of £250 after just two years. From 1869-89 a series of twenty-six reprinted editions were issued, each one carefully supervised by Dodgson and, where the illustrations were concerned, by Tenniel. As the audience of admirers widened, many translations into other languages followed, several of these also overseen by the author. The witty, challenging text, filled with puns, literary jokes and parodies of such famous poets as Southey and Wordsworth, appealed to adults as well as children. Christina

Rossetti wrote to offer Dodgson 'a thousand and one thanks ... for the funny pretty book you have so very kindly sent me. My Mother and Sister as well as myself made ourselves quite at home yesterday in Wonderland: and ... I confess it would give me sincere pleasure to fall in with that conversational rabbit, that endearing puppy, that very sparkling dormouse ... The woodcuts are charming.' Her brother Dante Gabriel Rossetti commented that 'The wonderful ballad of Father William and Alice's perverted snatches of school poetry are among the funniest things I have seen for a long while.' The book's admirers included Queen Victoria herself; the legend persists that, having read it with great enjoyment, she asked that the author's next work should be sent to her and was not amused when this turned out to be a geometry text book entitled *An Elementary Treatise on Determinants.*

The cherished image of the 'real' Alice remained with Dodgson for the rest of his life. Throughout his later years, and despite numerous new 'child-friends', his greatest consolation was to summon up the memory of the 'happy summer days' spent with her and her sisters. One of their last meetings took place on 25 June 1870, when Alice was eighteen years old. Mrs Liddell brought her, with Lorina, to be photographed in Dodgson's new set of college rooms. The photograph of Alice shows a solemn, unsmiling young woman, formally dressed, her hair neatly pinned up, staring rather bleakly into the camera lens — a striking contrast to the charming, eager, animated little girl in the portraits taken ten years earlier. [27]

A year later, on 4 May 1871, Dodgson wrote in his diary: 'On ... Alice's birthday, I sit down to record the events of the day, partly as a specimen of my life now ...'. In December of that year his sequel to Wonderland, *Through the Looking-Glass, and What Alice Found There* (once again illustrated by Tenniel) was published, and the first thing Dodgson did when he received his advance copies was to send three over to the Deanery, 'the one for Alice being in morocco'. The new story, describing Alice's adventures as she moves symbolically from child to adult in another magical world entered through the mirror in her Oxford drawing-room, drew together many anecdotes, events and ideas from different points in its author's life: the framework of a living chess game, for instance, probably makes use of private jokes and incidents from the days when Dodgson was teaching the Liddell children to play chess; the ideas based on mirror reversal — the White Queen's 'backward' memory, Alice's puzzlement at the notion that she has to walk away from an object in order to go towards it — arise from his fascination with logical inversion. The book was prefaced by a distinctly mournful poem dedicated to the 'child of the pure unclouded brow' he so fondly remembered:

27 Dodgson's last photograph of Alice, 1870

I have not seen thy sunny face
Nor heard thy silver laughter;
No thought of me shall find a place
In thy young life's hereafter -
Enough that now thou wilt not fail
To listen to my fairy-tale.

Other publications by 'Lewis Carroll' appeared during the period when Dodgson was preparing *Through the Looking-Glass* for publication. Shortly after his return from his only trip abroad, an expedition to Russia with a Christ Church colleague in the summer of 1867, his fairy story 'Bruno's Revenge' was published in the popular children's periodical *Aunt Judy's Magazine.* (His less accessible novel for adults and older children, *Sylvie and Bruno*, appeared over twenty years later.) *Phantasmagoria*, his first book of collected verse — containing both comic and serious poems — appeared in 1869, and a collection of his Oxford pamphlets came out, under his real name, in 1874, the same year as the long, mysterious nonsense poem *The Hunting of the Snark.* A retelling of the Wonderland story, in a shortened and simplified version for children below the age of five entitled *The Nursery Alice*, was published in 1889.

Meanwhile, Dodgson continued to spend time with various child-friends, Oxford colleagues and a growing circle of celebrated public figures; he often visited Guildford, where his family had moved from Yorkshire, took summer lodgings by the sea at Eastbourne, and made regular trips to London to visit exhibitions and see plays (including various stage productions of the *Alice* stories). He maintained a vast correspondence with children and adults, meticulously logged in a register which finally recorded over 100,000 letters sent and received. As he passed through his forties, however, he became increasingly concerned with accomplishing his academic work in mathematics and logic, and the tenor of his life became more austere.

In the summer of 1880, when Alice was twenty-eight, she was married, in Westminster Abbey, to Reginald Hargreaves, the only son of a wealthy mill owner and property magnate from Lancashire, who had been been educated at Eton and Christ Church. Five years after her marriage, Dodgson wrote to 'Alice-Liddell-that-was', as he described her in his diary. The letter began: 'I fancy this will come to you almost like a voice from the dead, after so many years of silence, but my mental picture is still as vivid as ever of one who was, through so many years, my ideal child-friend.' It went on to ask 'whether you have any objection to the original manuscript book of Alice's Adventures (which I suppose you still possess) being published in facsimile? ... I think, considering the extraordinary popularity the books have had (we have sold more than 120,000 of the two) there must be many who would like to see the original form.'

Alice consented to this request, and sent him her treasured manuscript. Dodgson wrote five more times in the next twenty months, reporting the progress of the facsimile and discussing various details concerning the preface and the use of the profits, which he suggested should go to a children's hospital. The book appeared as *Alice's Adventures Under Ground* in 1886; Alice received a copy inscribed 'To Her, whose namesake one happy summer day inspired his story: from the Author, Xmas 1886'.

Dodgson died twelve years later, on 14 January 1898, of a sudden attack of bronchial pneumonia which struck during the Christmas holiday with his family in Guildford, while he was working hard on the second volume of his *Symbolic Logic*. He had often contemplated death and accepted its approach without fear, writing to one of his sisters in 1896: 'It is getting increasingly difficult now to remember *which* of one's friends remain alive, and *which* have gone "into the land of the great departed, into the silent land". Also, such news comes as less and less of a shock, and more and more one realises that it is an experience each of *us* has to face before long ...'. He left instructions that his funeral be 'simple and inexpensive, avoiding all things which are merely done for show'. Many good friends and colleagues attended it, but no members of the Liddell family. His relatives cleared his Christ Church rooms, burning many papers, letters and manuscripts, but retaining a few of his possessions for themselves. In May an auction was held in Oxford of many of his beloved gadgets, games, puzzles, books, furniture, portraits, paintings and sketches, photographs, albums and cameras – all knocked down to the highest bidder.

Alice, however, continued to treasure the manuscript story of her 'adventures' until 1928 when, aged seventy-five, widowed and faced with substantial death duties, she put it up for sale at Sotheby's, in London. 'Lewis Carroll' was by now a name revered throughout the world, his manuscripts and inscribed first editions eagerly sought by rich collectors. The auction was held on 3 April, and Alice herself attended to see the little book purchased for £15,000 – a record price at that time – by an American dealer, Dr Rosenbach, who took it back with him to Philadelphia and sold it on to a wealthy collector, Eldridge Johnson, president of the Victor Talking Machine Company. In Christ Church Library there is a collection of press-cuttings commenting on the auction sale, and a letter from Alice to her son Caryl, excitedly describing the events of the day.

She resumed her by now rather lonely existence at Cuffnells , the Hargreaves family house in Hampshire; two of her three sons had been tragically killed in action in the Great War, and the third had moved away. In 1932, however, her life changed dramatically when, at eighty years old, she was invited to New York, to attend the lavish Lewis Carroll centenary celebrations at Columbia University, accompanied by her son Caryl and sister Rhoda. Here she was treated as a celebrity: admirers of the *Alice* books queued up to pay homage to her, she appeared in a Paramount newsreel, addressed the American people on the radio, wrote an article for the *New York Times* and received an honorary doctorate of letters. The remaining two years of her life were filled with new activity – answering letters about Lewis Carroll, making public appearances, unveiling memorials – until she was finally moved to confess to her son that she was 'tired of being Alice in Wonderland'.

In 1946, following the death of its American owner, the original Alice manuscript again came up for auction, in New York. Rosenbach again bought it, this time for $50,000. A plan was then hatched, however, by the prominent bibliophile Lessing Rosenwald, who persuaded a group of wealthy benefactors that the famous little book should be returned to its own country, as a gesture of thanks for the British people's gallantry in the Second World War. On 6 November 1948 the Librarian of Congress sailed for England on the *Queen Elizabeth*, taking the manuscript with him (and occasionally sleeping with it under his pillow). On 12 November he presented it to the British Museum 'as an expression of thanks to a noble people who kept Hitler at bay for a long period single-handed'. The Archbishop of Canterbury, who accepted it on behalf of the nation, acclaimed this gesture as 'an unsul-

28 A photograph of Alice aged eighty, in New York

lied and innocent act in a distracted and sinful world' – a sentiment which would have appealed to the story's creator.

Visitors from all over the world continue to flock to Christ Church in search of Lewis Carroll and Alice. Dodgson's sitting room is now a graduate common room: its original appearance is preserved only in a photograph. His William de Morgan fireplace tiles, with their strange creatures reminiscent of Wonderland, have been made into a fire screen which is now in the Senior Common Room. In the Great Hall, where one of the stained-glass windows is dedicated to Dodgson and Alice, hangs a rather sombre portrait of him, painted after his death. Alice's younger sister Edith, who died suddenly and tragically at the age of twenty-two, is commemorated as St Catherine in a beautiful memorial window, by Burne-Jones, in the Cathedral. In the Library is Alice's son Caryl Hargreaves's collection of hundreds of editions of the 'Alice' stories, in many languages, together with a fascinating hoard of 'Wonderland' and 'Looking-Glass' toys, games and memorabilia. The college also possesses a few of the 'real' Alice's possessions, some of them – gloves, fan, playing cards – strangely evocative of Dodgson's 'fairy tale' of long ago, the original version of which is now one of the greatest treasures on display in the British Library's exhibition galleries.

NOTE 'Alice's Adventures Under Ground' is British Library Additional MS 46700. Charles Dodgson's diaries are British Library Additional MSS 54340-54348

29
Dodgson's
illustration
of the trial scene

30
(*opposite*)
Dodgson's
illustration of
Alice with the
Queen of Hearts

"The Queen of Hearts she made some tarts
      All on a summer day:
The Knave of Hearts he stole those tarts,
      And took them quite away!"

"Now for the evidence," said the King, "and
then the sentence."

"No!" said the
Queen, "first the
sentence, and then
the evidence!"

"Nonsense!" cried
Alice, so loudly that
everybody jumped,
"the idea of having
the sentence first!

"Hold your
tongue!" said the Queen.

"I won't!" said Alice, "you're nothing but a
pack of cards! Who cares for you?"

At this the whole pack rose up into the
air, and came flying down upon her: she gave
a little scream of fright, and tried to beat
them off, and found herself lying on the bank,
with her head in the lap of her sister, who was
gently brushing away some leaves that had
fluttered down from the trees on to her face.

Further Reading

Anne Clark, *The Real Alice*, London, 1981

Morton N. Cohen (ed.), *The Letters of Lewis Carroll*, London, 1979

Morton N. Cohen, *Lewis Carroll, a Biography.*, London, 1995

Martin Gardner (ed.), *The Annotated Alice*, Harmondsworth, Penguin Books, 1970

Roger Lancelyn Green (ed.), *The Diaries of Lewis Carroll*, London, 1953

Robert Phillips, *Aspects of Alice*, Harmondsworth, Penguin Books, 1974

Acknowledgements

The following illustrations are reproduced by kind permission of Mrs M.J. St Clair: 1, 3, 4, 5, 6, 27, and 28.

Front cover illustration Dodgson's drawing of Alice with the White Rabbit

Back cover illustration Alice 'opening out like the largest telescope that ever was'

Half-title page illustration Dodgson's drawing of Alice with her sister at the opening of Chapter I

Frontispiece Title page from 'Alice's Adventures Under Ground'

© 1997 The British Library Board
First published 1997 by The British Library
Great Russell Street
London WC1B 3DG

ISBN 0 7123 4533 7

Designed and typeset in Monotype Centaur by Roger Davies

Colour origination by York House Graphics

Printed in Italy by Artegrafica, Verona